R Y

raymond youngblood version

I0158711

FAITH

THE FIRST BOOK OF
THE BOOK OF RAYMOND

Large Print Compact Edition

DR. RAYMOND YOUNGBLOOD, JR.

The Book
OF RAYMOND

TO:

_____

_____

_____

_____

BY:

_____

_____

_____

_____

M: _____ D: _____ Y:_____

Family: _____

_____

_____

_____

Publishing by **YOUNGBLOOD**

P.O. Box 230   P.O. BOX 525   P.O. BOX 200281
Pelican, Louisiana 71063   10 Monrovia 1000   CRA 44 N⁰ 48-79/Oficina 9-616
United States   Liberia   Medellin-Colombia

PUBLISHINGBYYOUNGBLOOD@GMAIL.COM
+1.318.755.2600

http://dryoungblood.tumblr.com TUMBLR
http://drraymondyoungbloodjr.wordpress.com WORDPRESS
google.com/+DrRaymondYoungbloodJr GOOGLE+
www.linkedin.com/in/drraymondyoungbloodjr LINKEDIN
facebook.com/DrRaymondYoungbloodJr FACEBOOK
http://www.pinterest.com/drryoungblood PINTEREST
https://twitter.com/DrYoungblood TWITTER
YOUNGBLOODSTVNETWORK YOUTUBE
http://flickr.com/drraymondyoungbloodjr FLICKR
publishingbyyoungblood@gmail.com email

R Y V Large Print Compact Edition

Library of Congress Cataloging-in-Publication Data
Youngblood, Jr., Raymond
Faith The First Book Of The Book Of Raymond//Raymond Youngblood, Jr.

Designed by Dr. Raymond Youngblood, Jr., DBA

THIS PARTICULAR E-BOOK OR PRINTED COPYBOOK ONLY CONTAINS
FAITH THE FIRST BOOK OF THE BOOK RAYMOND IN THIS. THE BOOK
OF RAYMOND CONSISTS OF TEN SEPARATE BOOKS.

New Version 2014

ISBN-10: 0986217735 (pb)   ISBN-13: 978-0-9862177-3-9 (pb)

ISBN-10: 0986217743 (eb)   ISBN-13: 978-0-9862177-4-6 (eb)

PBY: 000-000-000-000-2

Printed in the United States Of America

The Books of The Book Of Raymond

FAITH THE *FIRST* BOOK OF RAYMOND

SELF(YOU) THE *SECOND* BOOK OF RAYMOND

EMOTION THE *THIRD* BOOK OF RAYMOND

PROFESSIONAL THE *FOURTH* BOOK OF RAYMOND

RELATIONSHIP THE *FIFTH* BOOK OF RAYMOND

LIFE / DEATH THE *SIXTH* BOOK OF RAYMOND

ECONOMIC THE *SEVENTH* BOOK OF RAYMOND

PEOPLE THE *EIGHTH* BOOK OF RAYMOND

NATURE THE *NINTH* BOOK OF RAYMOND

SUPER NATURAL THE *TENTH* BOOK OF RAYMOND

CONTENTS

FAITH
The First Book Of

THE BOOKS FOR
STABILITY, FOCUS & PEACE

Reading the Book Of Raymond should inspire a positive life. This positive life shall include you, your family and the society in which you live.

All verses in the Book Of Raymond make no permanent reference to any particular belief. The Book encourages that all persons to use a common focal point to gain strong feelings toward themselves and all life form.

Where the word God is used has no reflection on any particular religion, practice or belief. It is used in an understanding that this particular book's original language is English and God is used as one's belief can make reference to a final destination or power to create or power to destroy or power to benefit.

The understanding of, The Book Of Raymond, shall be that any person, no matter color, creed, gender, sexual preference, sex, age, education, or ideology, shall find some form to gain Faith.

No one can be assigned Faith; it must be accepted in one's own time and will. At this time, this New Version shall be the only testimony of Faith, the First Book Of Raymond.

The capital use of the word "Faith" is meant to signify this particular book's focus.

All verses in this New Version make no reference to any one particular method that a person must pray, worship, or share a method. The Book Of Raymond only urges that a person shalt pray, worship, and share a method.

All verses in the Book Of Raymond have no prophecies and savior of humankind. You shall find your own way to what makes you worthy. This New Version does not refer to a leader or savior of a particular group, but creates cause in a way for a person or persons to find the way by liberating themselves with like minds.

Where God is mentioned, it is within the persons' own self, faith, and tribulations, there shall be recognition. A person shall choose to share the recognition with persons alike. The Book Of Raymond offers no support towards any person, no matter their belief or message, to force or maneuver any person's belief. A person's belief shalt be their own. Their own can only be shared, not forced.

In instances for translation, whether through vocabulary, vernacular, or definition, a teacher or student shalt not fabricate, but use common sense to explain. This is why this New Version is moderate in storytelling.

The beginning of every section is indicated by a verse number. A verse shall be read in full to ensure it is ease of comprehension and leads to a clearer understanding.

The Book Of Raymond extracts life lessons from many teachers. It offers to contribute to all learners those that teach a person who is humane to all creatures, beings, and life forms.

The Book Of Raymond reveals multifaceted forms of beliefs, which is allows you to change during a person's human growth, experiences, relationships, and feelings.

The Book Of Raymond, make attempts to clarify the complexities and chooses to use common simple language to help in translation.

Where you read and do not understand, nor do you understand in translation, please continue to read, for the Book Of Raymond is like life, the more you endure, the better you understand. Re-read an area if you have to. Try to retain the information for your own growth.

There are no must do's, have to's, and don'ts prior to reading. Feel free to open to any page, feel free to purify before touching the book, feel free in any situation. Keep in mind that cleanliness is a virtue respected by all.

Record your readings and understandings. Record the discussion of different teachers (a teacher may be anyone, a teacher has no educational boundaries). Different teachers offer a wide variety of understanding and different points of view. Compare what you learned.

Place a bookmark where needed, read a section multiple times and over time. The length of each Book Of Raymond was chosen for the purpose of enlightening a person's approaches toward human growth and development.

In your own time seek refuge; it helps protect you from attacks, be it literal, or be it spiritual. When in silent prayer or open prayer feel free to recite positive words that open hearts and minds. Try not to interrupt others while in prayer and place yourself in a position to not be interrupted.

No day shall be designated to read or study. Choose your days as an individual or as a group.

Enunciate every letter and word, to capture the essence and understanding.

The Book Of Raymond does not mention heaven or hell as a destination for any life form.

A miracle shall be a miracle. A blessing shall be a blessing. Work shall be work. Prayer, worship, and sharing of teaching without the physical work are not to be considered a gain or loss. Once you finish praying, then you must go and literally do the work associated with the prayers.

Say the truth in your prayers, say the truth in your heart, and your message will have many messengers.

Books in The Book Of Raymond have measured life that you will be born, you will live, then you will die. You shall fill your life with purpose and these purposes shall come at different times and different stages.

You shall use the Books to help your persona; prosperity in this world. Enjoy growth, enjoy people, enjoy pleasures, and enjoy any form of wisdom for it offers advantages.

Remember a wicked tongue may receive something different from an aggressive tongue; wicked ways may receive something different from aggressive ways. No action is absent and no reaction is equal.

Every person and being has one life; therefore, it shall be respected and protected by all.

Another person's belief shall have the same respect as your own, whether in agreement and/or disagreement.

Take your time and read to absorb.

Read according to your time and feelings. Make no worries how long it takes to read. Focus on understanding what you read. Focus on applying what you understand.

Read alone, read in a group, have others read to you, and you read to others, read to children and have children read to others; this will bring many different meanings and this is wonderful.

TheBookOfRaymond

The First Book of Raymond, Called

FAITH

The First Book Of Raymond, called Faith, focuses on Faith through the stages of human growth and understanding multiple facets of one's faith in society and how we are so divided that faith in self and others is becoming out of reach to the entire world. The second part focuses on positive faith in one's own faith and non-faith, one not having in accordance to classical faith beliefs. In the world and the path at which we are each traveling seems to be limiting our days. The use of boundaries that people of the world are putting up across color, religion, age, races, tribe, ethnicity, economic status, culture, land, water, space (air), social status, education and gender have placed the entire world in jeopardy.

Faith is an English word having etymology of Anglo-French/Latin meaning trust or to trust, complete trust or confidence in someone or something or strong belief.

1

1:1 In the beginning a man and a woman created you.

1:2 And you were without form and shape; and in total darkness while in the womb. Measured through a woman's menstrual cycle of exactly 28-days prior to pregnancy; a spontaneous onset of labor; the mean pregnancy length estimated at 283.4 days of gestational age; timed from the first day of the last menstrual period as recalled by the woman; and with a natural occurrence and blessing you moved from a woman's flesh; you move from the water and the darkness.

1:3 And there was light; there was sound; there was taste; there was smell; there was touch; you were born.

1:4 And you will not know the meaning of the days, nor the meaning of the night, after many months you would know that light is good and understand the light from the darkness.

1:5 And, as you understand more, you will understand the light of Day and the darkness of Night.

1:6 In hardship the evening can start a new day and the morning of every day will be the first day for a new start. Your sleep will be without any sense of time and direction, for you will only know awake or sleep.

1:7 And you will come to know many things: of food and hunger, sweet and bitter, hot and cold, wet and dry, soft and hard, crawling and walking, helpful and helpless. All of these things at this stage are without meaning and appreciation from you.

1:8 And as you develop in movement, size, recognition, and observance, you start to separate and create short-term and long-term memory.

1:9 Your selfishness will be relentless, as it will contribute to your survival.

1:10 You will cry for feeding, you will cry when you soil yourself, you will cry when sleep moves upon you. Crying brings attention to you, it becomes your first form of communication, even before laughter.

1:11 And if you are a boy or a girl, it matters not.

1:12 And experiences are building you and your persona through what you like and dislike. In the beginning it is simple.

1:13 You first learn the speech of one to fifty words.

1:14 You experience forms of levels of anxiety.

1:15 And you will know all this before you know your mother is your mother and your father is your father.

1:16 You will not understand grandmother or grandfather, brother or sister, aunt or uncle, cousins or friends, regardless of who they are, this will matter not.

END

FAITH

1ST VERSE NOTES:

FAITH

2

2:1 Thus, your growth and experience are forming and all that you do will form your permanent mind and ways; this is without your knowing or understanding.

2:2 Your skin is sensitive, crying, sucking noise, teething, rolling over, can point to objects; this will consume you.

2:3 Now reaching, creeping, crawling and throwing-this because of your new found development and begins a new level of need; and yet you cannot understand the word "no" or even danger.

2:4 You are without ignorance and stupidity for anything you do is without fault; without responsibilities; without ownership; free from judgment; free from judging others.

2:5 And at age two you can chew with teeth. A tooth (plural teeth) is a small, calcified, whitish structure found in the jaw or mouth, in particular, yours will come at the front of your mouth.

2:6 In the beginning the growth of your tooth will be your first stage of how well you self-consume pain and annoyance known as teething. This means nothing to you for later in life teeth signify health and longevity and freedom from disease; this means nothing to you.

2:7 You will start your transition from sucking and gnawing and use the teeth to break down food; food becomes another reliance of selfishness without your control; choosing the type, sweet, bitter, spicy, textures, salty becomes selfish acts later referred to as desire.

2:8 No act of being selfish is more so than faith of which you have absolutely none; you're only having freedom from burden of maintaining faith.

2:9 And at age two you can walk around, recognize expressions and pain, use the pronoun I or me, make demands, and express curiosity about the world.

2:10 Walking around becomes a freedom of movement, sense or senseless direction as all movement is curiosity, need, want and commands. No movement is without somebody's level of selfishness. For you, no movement is without faith whether you recognize it to be so or not. At this point any acts of harm you avoid will be attached to luck and not faith.

2:11 Luck (or chance) differs by whom is describing it by religious, philosophical, mystical, or emotional context or whoever is interpreting it in accordance to the event or situation; according to the classic or classical definition luck is without purpose and is with absolutely no control in any matter, event, or situation in favor of or unfavorable to a cause, individual, group, thing, principal, or aims. When educated, a person recognizes that a particular incident will be a

person or thing that gives rise to an action known as a phenomenon or accident or condition. No influences should dismiss control or no influences shall dismiss itself. All this matters not as faith as it is still not recognized as faith.

2:12 And at age three your body is coming into form as your neck **protrudes** exceeds from your shoulders; you can move great distances from safety; you can listen to what interests you; and can ask questions associated with events. You can ask, "What are you doing? What is this?"

Not now, but at some point, a question will be, "What do you believe in?"

2:13 And at age four you can listen and take commands, walk in a straight line, paint and draw, read, be friendly or not, have mood changes, boast or lie (story telling), cooperate, establish relationships, and be selfish and tattle on others' wrong doing. At this stage it is not envy or jealously with recognition by you.

2:14 And if you are a boy or a girl, it matters not, you are still without faith, you are still without recognition of faith. Your faith shall remain with your caretaker. A caretaker has nothing to do with mother or father, but for anyone who cares for your well-being.

2:15 And at age five you can walk, run, jump; you can control your pencil and construct objects and count; you understand light and dark; you know jokes, time and calendar; your vocabulary is more than 1,500 words with past tense and present tense uses.

2:16 Though you are without recognizing faith, it's ironic you can know and have a sense of guilt when you lie, steal or commit a bad act.

2:17 And at age six your permanent teeth will form, your eye sight is 20/20, you can make things, tie things, fold things and help. You can experiment with words, show enthusiasm, and be of an inquisitive behavior, anxious to please, not knowing morals, not being ethical, but knowing bad things.

2:18 And at the seventh year (*ironically, matched with seven days in a week*), you definitely know right from wrong; you can comprehend and reason; you definitely have a sense of guilt and of being shameful.

2:19 You know not of luck and not of faith.

2:20 And as a child, thou learnt attachment and predictability, autonomy and security, differentiation and influence, affiliation and respect.

2:21 You start to play and knowingly experiment with body parts.

2:22 And as a child you have come to understand basic trust versus mistrust, virtue of hope with an appreciation of people (*mother, father and family*).

2:23 You know facial expressions and body language of adults. You understand patterns of behavior whether innocence, whether violence, whether kindness.

2:24 And as a child you have come to know moral responsibility versus shame, a virtue of will with an acceptance of the human lifecycle.

2:25 And as a child you have come to recognize initiative versus guilt, a virtue of purpose with being humorous, knowing empathy and resilience.

2:26 And as a pre-adolescent of nine years to twelve years, thou know-thou-self and acknowledge feelings, understand feelings, and combine behavior and affection, reading people and understanding role models.

2:27 And as a pre-adolescent you have come to be aware of industry versus inferiority with a virtue of competence with an acceptance of humility.

2:28 And faith.

2:29 And as an adolescent of thirteen to eighteen years, thou can build external identity, trust yourself, take risks, and assess dangers of the world versus balancing of boundaries and acceptance of action.

2:30 The expectation of adult behavior shall be expected the more constant you are with this behavior, the more others feel your most selfish act of being on your own will be to your advantage. The caretakers sense of value to your accomplishments is measured through what is form and tolerated of your maturity.

2:31 And as an adolescent one understands identity versus confusion, a virtue of fidelity with a sense of complex things, logic, an appreciation of beauty and not beautiful, and understands physical attributes.

2:32 Whereas you are not of legal age, all physical acts are under the refuge of your parents, you have not reached the age of moral reasoning. You, your age, your faults, your wrongs, and your ways on social judgment will reflect on thou parents; you shall be the responsibility of your parents; shalt not you depend on this, as in reality, some man made laws (*judicial system*) have punished even those underage.

2:33 And in early adulthood of eighteen to twenty-five years, thou understand intimacy versus isolation, a virtue of love, with a sense of the level relationships become complex, and the values of loving freely and having tenderness are known to you. Emotions make up a great portion of your body's reaction and feelings; you are of age and should feel free to physically love; feel free to safely have sex with no limits of legal ramifications and public ridicule. It is expected, and to some degree accepted.

2:34 By some it is expected to be married and by others it is expected to just be safe as willing partners.

2:35 By some it is expected to be a man and woman and by others it is expected to just be safe as willing partners.

2:36 A person with true faith has no limitations of sex and anyone persons orientation; for the orientation has little to do with character; for character is the actual results and focus.

2:37 And in adulthood of twenty-six to sixty-four years thou understand generatively versus stagnation, a virtue of care, with unconditional love, empathy, and concerns and caring for other people.

2:38 Your faith will be at the highest strength, the lowest focus and most influential. Your faith shall be measured according to the accomplishments and failures as an individual, family, and group settings. You recognize, and with confidence, trade the word *luck*, with *faith* and in some instances use both. For at this stage in life a sense of family can start to consume.

2:39 And if you are a boy or a girl, it matters.

2:40 And in the latter stages of life at the age of sixty-five to death, thou understand honesty versus hopelessness, a virtue of wisdom, with human-to-human identity, and integrity strong enough to take physical strength.

2:41 You begin the stages of reverting back to childhood through memories and in some cases we refer to this stage as a crisis, thus depending solely on your failures.

2:42 You purposely impose faith onto others and you offer others to contribute to your faith.

2:43 Faith becomes more than a belief that needs no proof or trust.

2:44 You accept and you believe where no explanation is needed.

2:45 It is safe for you to take the worse situations and consider that it can improve.

2:46 Faith becomes a part of your ethics and morals. It becomes a part of your personality.

2:47 Others can even use it to benefit your needs or use your faith in a sense of guilt to gain for themselves.

2:48 It becomes a sense of trust that defines itself through your confidence of others, information, situations or your trust in a person whether it's a priest, imam, bishop, rabbi, pastor, preacher, apostle, educator or professional.

2:49 You trust your faith and educate through a deity, views, or in the doctrines or teachings of a religion and non-religious factors.

2:50 Faith is not a miracle, for a miracle is in the form of a single act.

2:51 Faith becomes trust, hope, and belief.

END

FAITH

2ND VERSE NOTES:

_____   _____
_____   _____
_____   _____
_____   _____
_____   _____
_____   _____
_____   _____
_____   _____
_____   _____
_____   _____
_____   _____
_____   _____
_____   _____
_____   _____
_____   _____
_____   _____
_____   _____
_____   _____
_____   _____
_____   _____
_____   _____
_____   _____
_____   _____
_____   _____
_____   _____
_____   _____
_____   _____
_____   _____
_____   _____
_____   _____

FAITH

3

3:1 Thou have passed many stages in life; you are fully aware of the day and night; right and wrong.

3:2 Thou hath learnt survival and all that you have been called upon to do. You shall know that a calling is also associated to your survival and well-being.

3:3 Thou learnt to care, and learnt to overcome turmoil, and learnt love, and learnt heartaches from the loss of love ones.

3:4 Thou will cook and clean; find a dwelling place (a home); further educate thy self of human principles; gain talent to feed thyself; have children; be prosperous in wealth, life, and happiness.

3:5 This shall not be the same for all who live. Though it is morally and financially possible, norms of a society are not of interest to the majority to accomplish this level of living. So we separate into our own level of being prosperous in wealth, life and happiness.

3:6 Faith is one of life's only means of being equal, but physical prospering is a combination of faith, strategy, and labor.

3:7 Therefore, your parents will know when you have come of age; they have walked this path before you.

3:8 Therefore, thou should grasp the wisdom and talents of thou parents (*caretakers*): For two roads diverged in the forest, one road looked heavily traveled, the other is covered with thick brush. Thou parents know the reason why the road covered in brush is least traveled. You are wise to seek their advice. You are stupid to seek their bosom after you enter the brush.

3:9 Thou parent's bosom can never shield you from the ills of society; it is only your maturity, it is only your faith.

3:10 If you and your parents refuse to place you in society with good moral behavior, society will determine thy age; society will be responsible for your doings and doings not.

3:11 Whereas you are under the excessive refuge of your parents refusing to leave their bosom, it matters not; society judges you on your age, your faults, your wrongs, your ways, and the previous behavior and judgments of others; this will not reflect on thou parents; it will reflect you.

3:12 Whereas you are of age, "therefore," said your parents, "My child is of age, ask him."

3:13 Therefore when asked your age, a person shall be of certain expectation of your behavior, maturity, knowledge and "know with all".

3:14 When thou hear the question, "What is thou age?" If an adult by science, but a child by mind, you will be embarrassed, if the child is fully capable. Where the child is with a birth defect, defect of the mind or by accident this shall be accepted no matter the age for the child is without responsibility.

3:15 You shall still be held accountable for any action by law or by societal beliefs. This will matter not what your faith is, but the faith of those who stand as your judge.

3:16 Whereas if you hear the question, "What is thy age?" Know that thou who ask are reasoning with expectations of you.

3:17 Different societies across the world have their own standards, it matters not, as all societies are becoming uniform to protect human development of girls and boys and men and women.

3:18 And it is possible that some mothers and fathers lack an ability to instill morals. It is also possible that the child-to-adult wish is not to have good morals.

3:19 Some persons maybe without good moral character, no matter the upbringing or support, for the chemical imbalance of the mind does not correlate with society.

3:20 Your behavior can determine your societal respect, despite thy age.

3:21 When no one is aware of your age and you want to deceive, society will utilized science, and you will be judged through a scientific and organic law.

3:22 And it matters not if you are a man (male) or woman (female).

3:23 Thou father and mother is to release you into society whether they agree or not; you do right, you will stand; you do wrong, you will stand. You will face judgment.

3:24 Thou know of right, thou know of wrong; thou hath or hath not faith.

3:25 And it came to pass after all these experiences and things of learning, you are in acceptance of yourself and your faith.

3:26 You will say, "Behold world, here I am."

3:27 No one shall stand for you at a certain point in life, for it will be you and your faith.

3:28 You will be free to do the same for your child.

3:29 Your child will be free to do the same for their child and so on.

3:30 It shall be the concern of the child to care for their parents. It becomes the responsibility of the young to see to the needs of the old, therefore the young shall gain the knowledge of the old in exchange for care.

3:31 A parent shall be understanding of their children financial means and capabilities while receiving care.

3:32 Multiple children should combine resources in the care of parents.

3:33 No elderly person shall hold on to any life lessons or technical knowledge; the knowledge shall be passed on to their children, family or any other person's child.

END

FAITH

3RD VERSE NOTES:

FAITH

4

4:1 Faith, sent down upon you is truth, confirming what was before and what is to come.

4:2 And your faith is to reveal what is to come.

4:3 No one faith will decide your faith for you and faith will be one; for if you have faith, then you will know your faith.

4:4 And your faith will be your own directly connected for the entire existence.

4:5 What is thou faith? Thou faith is not betwixt, nor between, any other persons and self. Thou faith is thou own.

4:6 Accept thou faith as thy own and thou will prosper in many ways. It matters not though which format; have faith. No religion shall determine your faith no matter the consequences of other's belief. It is most important to be of good behavior and useful to others.

4:7 Faith is a guidance for the people; faith is a guidance for you. Indeed, those who disbelieve will be left to deal with their own severe punishments or prosperities.

4:8 And it is not for you to judge anyone's faith and method of praise. To conquer your own trust and faith, you have until your death; only then can your belief and strength of faith be determined. At no time, should you judge others.

4:9 And it is not for you to decide retribution for another person's faith. To form retribution takes away the lifetime you need to fully develop your own faith.

4:10 And it is not faith to harm a person based on what they believe. Where thou hast a belief that your faith shall lead you to harm others, due to how they have faith and how they worship, thou shall start with thyself. If you want to cut off their hands and feet; thou should cut off all thou own hands and feet first. If thou want others to be blind, thou should remove thou own head first. Harm to be committed to others is not acceptable because of how they worship.

4:11 Indeed, nothing is hidden in the world, nor in faith.

4:12 It is thy mother and father who conceive your beginning and then thou formed in the womb; however, thou mother and father shall provide thy first understanding towards faith; if not, thou mother and father, and society shall provide the freedom to choose.

4:13 Through threats and castigation hold strong to what you believe and what you feel comfortable to believe.

4:14 In death the opinions of others will matter not. It is only your faith that matters.

4:15 There is no deity betwixt and between you and your faith.

4:16 Surely the people will assemble at different locations about which there is no doubt with no failures all promises will be kept. Once you can create your faith, you can accomplish your promise; you can complete your deeds.

4:17 Indeed, those who disbelieve shall seek out advice of persons with true faith.

4:18 Indeed, those who felt they did not receive morals from their home, it matters not; you shall place yourself to have and learn from a person with true faith. You shall trust yourself.

4:19 You have the ultimate freedom; to choose; to educate; to believe.

4:20 They are like customs and heritage of those before you. They are signs and learnt things that cannot be denied or go away.

4:21 Say to those who have no faith or their faith is not believed to be strong, "Hello!" Find something to discuss, never discuss or force anything upon them. You must reframe, for your positive attitude will invite them. It may take days or it may take till the second before death. Ask them not where they worship or pray. For this is luring. Ask for friendship. Be good and kind to each other. Be firm to each other when need be.

4:22 You must not castigate them, ridicule them, or harm them, for we are all of the same, from the same.

4:23 You are to respect them and in your form of worship and through your faith, speak of them with goodness and kindness. Wish for blessing for them. Wish for them to be prosperous. Do not stand in their path unless you offer freedom of which is not forced.

4:24 For we all need remember our faith is our own and our faith is direct; you will spend eternity developing the perfection of your relationship with your faith.

4:25 When someone comes to recruit you (*and they will*) into their faith, their way of thinking, their family, their army; feel a sense of freedom and honoring that they see the strength in you; your faith is your own and their faith is their own and no one shall have control of you as your faith is direct.

4:26 Again, when someone comes to recruit you (and they will) into their faith, their way of thinking, their family, their army; you do not feel a sense of freedom and honoring and that they see you as weak; do not be offended, feel great that your own faith has opened your vision and you saw the troubles or the blessings; just be mindful of their intention. Indeed in that is a lesson and a path and a blessing.

4:27 The enjoyment of worldly life is divided; your hard work must not go unrewarded, but remember to not lose your faith and humanness.

4:28 "Nothing is ever as good as you want it to be;" as can be said by many. Faith is as good and fulfilling as you want it to be; faith allows all to equal.

4:29 To gain something from what you deserve and you earned is a blessing; to gain otherwise is not wise. No deed, just cause or action, will remain unknown or unrecorded.

4:30 If what you found was not yours, then it belongs to someone else; therefore, it's someone else's.

4:31 Those who say, "indeed we have believed," so reward us, forgive us and protect us, will also be the ones who say, indeed we have been patient, truthful, obedient, helpful, and with faith.

4:32 Whenever those that were given the ability to enlighten others do anything to the contrary, you must not think bad against them. If the thing they have done is of harm in the physical or economical realm, place them before the law. If the thing they have done is of the spiritual, keep your faith; keep your faith strong, leave them to their faith.

4:33 No work is without equal and just pay. No faith will ask you to serve without a reward of some kind. Indeed, such a reward is not to be judged, if accepted with good intentions.

4:34 Those wearing of the same face mix in multiple faith, having faith, and not having faith, will point their life towards all those having faith in another, while showing another face. We are to consider this in our faith. To each their own is your relationship.

4:35 A good person selling in the market all day, you haggle the price of their goods; your relative whom is lazy and not deserving asks and you give; is that just? Your excuse is that they are family. Your excuse is the reason there shalt be no prosperity.

4:36 Nothing, absolutely nothing, is concealed; all there is to know, is known.

4:37 Believe in you, believe in your faith; believe in it. And no one will be reminded except those of understanding.

END

4TH VERSE NOTES:

FAITH

FAITH

5

5:1 Now, the choice of life shall also be represented with the consequences.

5:2 Your faith has an "enactability" to a self-prescribed path of life-long non-violence towards all living beings; and provides emphasis of spiritual independence and equality between all life-forms.

5:3 To practice non-violence and self-control are the means by which a person can obtain "constant-liberation".

5:4 You as a person, a being, a life-form, must learn to conquer, a never ending battle with 'passion' and 'pleasure' that you the individual will always undertake.

5:6 To have a passion to be the world's greatest, you put forth the commitment and efforts which is not the same as the want to sleep with a married person that you have not the rights, nor commitment. If you are to be a predator, know that as a predator you have no rights.

5:7 For some to have pleasure is to have a husband and wife loving each other with great joy and entangling in the pleasures of love and sex often; thus is the ultimate pleasure of committed people: is not the same as a rapist whom gains pleasure by preying on others.

5:8 Infinite knowledge, perception, powers and joy shall be achieved through your faith.

5:9 The soul of your faith retains an individual identity with you. This is the same as life. Sugar is sweet and vinegar is sour; a musical note is the same to any language and a number sounds different, but is of the same count, it matters not from where it comes for this is its identity.

5:10 Faith does not know of black people, white people, yellow people or brown people;

this is the beauty and respect of faith.

5:11 Any living being may become enlightened.

5:12 You can know that evil comes from many angles and wrongs. Evil can result from cravings, attachments, ignorance, greed, hatred and violence.

5:13 Evil can arise out of a non-true faith. Evil can rise from your overindulgence.

5:14 Salvation for oneself and extinguishing all attachments enables one to become enlightened; you find freedom in wisdom and wisdom can be liberating shielding a person from limits and offering them knowledge, power, and happiness.

5:15 One must follow the right faith, right knowledge, and right conduct.

5:16 What goes around, comes around; what you do to others, shall be done to you; for you shall not seek revenge, but you shalt allow yourself to be taken advantage of. Rely on the guilt or guilty conscience of theirs and not yours.

5:17 Suffering is a result of past activities, greed, hatred, poor planning, and ignorance, which returns as suffering.

5:18 Suffering is real and should not be seen as illusions. Suffering is one way of actively ridding oneself of bad intention.

5:19 You do wrong to other people and nothing you do will appear to go the way it is supposed to. Realize it is your conscience.

5:20 Love betwixt two people will lie heavily on their faith, regardless of their gender.

5:21 Your love for others will totally be based on your faith and your ability to love.

5:22 Celibacy is your right and your freedom; this shall go beyond the law. No path to faith and keeping faith is harder than staying on your own path.

5:23 Opulence (wealth) of faith is in some ways is expressed through joy, through prayer, through requested sharing; in some ways, it is not gain when a person refuses to except anything as faith, refusing to understand any form of direction, and refusing to savor those obstacles that block enlightenment; in some ways, it is inexpressible to share your faith or receive faith.

5:24 Life brings many things that can challenge your development of faith. This is where you have an opportunity to use the challenges as wisdom; this pain has an ability to endure mishaps as a chance to teach.

5:25 Wealth is the abundance of something; valuable resources and faith should be seen as an intangible form of wealth; possessing faith is simple; faith cannot be in abundance the same as material wealth. Faith is simple. Either you have faith or you need faith.

5:26 Giving of thou money to any house of worship shall be by thou own limits and heart. Feel no pressure, be under no authority, for you are giving based on what thou own house can afford.

END

5TH VERSE NOTES:

FAITH

6

6:1 Faith, will carry you when nothing else will.

6:2 Faith, shall be with morals.

6:3 Faith, shall be with ethics.

6:4 Faith, shall be with love.

6:5 Faith shall be with hope.

6:6 Faith, shall be with principles.

6:7 Faith, shall be with values.

6:8 Faith shall be belief and physical.

6:9 Faith shall not be without emotions.

6:10 Faith has no conditions.

6:11 Faith is not bound by a religion.

6:12 Faith is not bound by a single belief, but a common-wealth of beliefs.

6:13 Faith is not bound by a single way of life, but a commonwealth of ways of life.

6:14 Faith is more a way of life than a form of thought; the theist and the atheist, the skeptic and the agnostic are all created the same and by the same; their acceptance through their faith insists not on religious conformity, but on a spiritual and ethical outlook of life.

6:15 All is not a sect, but a fellowship of all who accept the law of right and are seriously seeking faith.

6:16 Faith is not a definite dogmatic creed, but a vast complex way to each individual, a subtly unified mass of spiritual beliefs that blends into realization.

6:17 Faith is not with spiritual as it has to start with the person and their norms. Spiritual comes when this is what the person decides.

6:18 Faith offer endeavors of the human spirit is continuously enlarging.

6:19 Faith is wholly free from strange obsessions and fake faiths. True faith is not just acceptance of particular metaphysical beliefs; one must believe for it is necessary for salvation.

6:20 Having no faith can lead to lack of love and emotions.

6:21 Faith is not bound up with creeds, or books, or prophets, or founders, or people laying claim to a calling.

6:22 Faith is the persistent search for truth and emotional bonding on the basis of a c o n t i n u o u s l y r e n e w e d experience.

6:23 A person's faith is in continuous evolution with God, remember the first time you experience having faith shall differ as growth strengthen your decision and your faith is without persuasion. Your faith

you shalt hold without bargain without compromise.

6:24 Faith is an inheritance of humble thoughts and aggressive aspiration, faithfully living and gracefully moving with the movement of you and life itself.

6:25 Faith has no boundaries.

6:26 Faith has no limits.

6:27 Faith exhibits a complete independence and freedom of the human mind.

6:28 Faith allows a person to have full confidence in their own capabilities.

6:29 With faith, a person has freedom.

6:30 The freedom is in thinking about God and other beliefs; it is your right and your right as an individual or group.

6:31 Your faith must endure life challenges until you are capable of reasoning.

6:32 Intuition that cannot be defined, is only to be experienced.

6:33 Evil and error are not final in a person's faith, for you must remember that true faith has no limits.

6:34 One can consider that there is no hell, because considering that means there is such a place where God is not, there are evil and wickedness which exceed faith and love.

6:35 When your faith is strong and unbreakable and you follow a path of belief, no other place can exist except where God is.

6:36 Praising is welcome worshiping that is within yourself.

6:37 For where your faith is with your own beliefs, know this is with no limits.

6:38 Faith, if true, shall consume a person's inner body, outer body, thoughts, mind, and physical actions along any path.

6:39 No action shall be the less and/or most colorful without faith and a person's faith shall be an endless diversity of hues.

6:40 For you to worry about how another person has face or worship, and bring yourself to worry if the person has an idol, means you have not totally understood faith and you are a distance from faith.

6:41 Faith takes a lifetime commitment; therefore, you should focus on your faith, as faith has provided multiple outlets for cultures to connect, true faith is faith, with no limits.

6:42 Faith shall not no know exclusive worship.

6:43 Faith will take to all forms of beliefs and reflections so you can gain.

6:44 Believers in their faith shall recognize groups or the authorities that lay claim to the only path; they shall remain strong in themselves. Faith has not one path.

6:45 Faith can recognize true prophets and seers of our existence and through such persons the fidelity (cause) to every layer and shade of truth as one knows it can be understood.

6:46 People are to affirm that there is a central reality, the one without a second, who is all that is and beyond all that is.

6:47 It is not unfaithful to recognize prophets and seers, for their ability can lift individuals and large groups, especially those who have no guidance.

6:48 For the lost, for the misguided, for the unknowing, the prophets and seers can help direct to a path; at this path the person is on their own to follow.

6:49 A person rising above the glamour of the fleshly life, material beliefs, find their pure pleasure of soul. A person with true faith can have the glamour of the fleshly life, material beliefs, and find their pure pleasure of soul.

6:50 For you are ever striving towards the divine, your thoughts are constantly turned to fresh illumination and spiritual recovery and recommencement. This is the place you want to be.

6:51 Faith should be appealing to us, not only by its thought and majestic vision, but also by its passion of devotion and sweetness of spiritual emotional enlightenment.

6:52 Faith recognizes that each religion is impossible to escape from, bound up with its culture, and can grow organically.

6:53 Faith can offer you a clean break away from troubles or give you a path towards a new direction, your own faith is freedom to express.

6:54 A person's faith helps them be aware that all religions have attained to some level of truth and goodness, and you can have faith without a religion, for faith is within yourself.   END

FAITH

6TH VERSE NOTES:

FAITH

7

7:1 Faith insists that people all have a right to express themselves.

7:2 Religions reform themselves by interpretations and adjustments to one another; you shall just keep a positive attitude and positive fellowship, not a negative tolerance. Feel not obligated to join a religion, though fellowshipping with others is joyous. For you can have a positive attitude and positive fellowship; not a negative tolerance with just faith alone.

7:3 Faith represents an effort at comprehension and cooperation.

7:4 Faith recognizes the diversity in a person's approach towards life, realization of life, and dealing with actual reality.

7:5 Faith is the essence of religion. It consists in a person's hold on what is eternal and existing in all being.

7:6 Faith is true.

7:7 If only a person adheres sincerely and honestly to follow faith, they get beyond the creed to the experience, beyond the formula to the vision of the truth.

7:8 Faith represents the spirit.

7:9 Your harmony between your body and spirit is within your soul, psyche, (*inner thinking*) self, inner being, ego, inner man/woman, mind.

7:10 Faith is not philosophy; faith is not just body and flesh.

7:11 Faith is not a spirit that haunts and it is not a ghost; it does not have anything to do with being a spook or spooking others. Thou should not feel scared and not make others feel scared through any means of faith. Faith is feeling comfort and at ease.

7:12 Faith goes beyond just an attitude, frame of mind, way of thinking, point of view, outlook, thoughts, ideas, mood, state of mind, emotional state, humor, and temper.

7:13 Prevailing faith goes beyond anything hindering your rights or others' rights, tendencies, moods, feelings, attitudes, beliefs, principles, standards and ethics.

7:14 Faith will give you a never ending level of courage, bravery, valor, strength of character, fortitude, backbone, determination, ability to create resolution, resolve dilemmas, fight, grit, guts, spunk, and sand. Faith will make you enter a dark room, a dark place, a dark feeling. Faith will give you control over your fears.

7:15 Faith offers a great spirit through enthusiasm, eagerness, keenness, liveliness, vivacity, energy, zest, panache, sparkle, exuberance, gusto, zeal, fire, passion; and informal get-up-and-go. Faith can give you swagger. Having true faith is bravery.

7:16 The spirit of faith is so real, true meaning, true intention, essence and substance.

7:17 To have the gift of faith has such extraordinary vitality as to survive norms as a professional, in politics and in society.

7:18 Faith alone can give our civilization a soul and men and women a principle to live by.

7:19 A person with true faith realizes not only that all roads lead to the one supreme whether in physical form, form or belief, but also that each person must choose that path which starts from the point at which they find themselves at the moment.

7:20 Faith is not going to allow your religious sense to speak rashly, which is displaying or proceeding from a lack of careful consideration of the possible consequences of an action; nor will it allow a profane word of anything which the soul of a person holds or has held sacred. You will have to earn what you gain.

7:21 Your faith is simple and does not have to be explained to any person or any group at any time during any setting. Never feel compelled to expose your faith; only feel joyous that others want to be a part.

7:22 One's attitude of respect for all creeds, this simple good manner in matters of spirit, is bred into the heart of every one, of every being.

7:23 Faith, includes, but is not limited to prayer, bowing, kneeling, hymns, lighting of candles, smoke, holy water, holy oils, fasting, meditating, confession, holy visions, or chanting, but faith also requires physical action. These actions are physical and can add to the enlightenment.

7:24 Faith is not without work.

7:25 Faith can guide you, it will not lead you.

7:26 Faith is without excuses, lies and complaints; if you have faith, then you have faith.

7:27 Faith is having peace.

7:28 Faith is without violence and cruelty.

7:29 Faith is without evil, jealousy, and wickedness.

7:30 Faith is beauty, truth, pure (of) heart, goodness, morality; for they are all connected; inseparable from each other.

7:31 Faith is having an aesthetic sensitivity, an emotional sensibility toward the world, and people with a sincere ear will hear.

7:32 Faith is its own strength, as for a non-faith person believes there is faith to have non-faith; for this is true, such a person will find faith, as all must find it as it is.

7:33 Faith is to exist; one and unique; being incorporeal; being eternal; focus faith; no law supersedes; all known and unknown thoughts and deeds of people are known; goodness is rewarded and evil is punished.

7:34 Faith must always be present; each individual's relationship is unique and personal.

7:35 Faith is knowing every person is equally important and has an infinite potential to do good in the world; equally important is not the same for those providing and those receiving the acts.

7:36 Faith allows a person to have the freewill to make choices in their lives and each person is responsible for the consequences of those choices.

7:37 When you find that excuses, lies, complaints, evil, jealousy, and wickedness are with you, though you continue to try and overcome these non-faith acts, know that all acts are freewill and the first step to a fruitful existence is accepting all actions and responsibilities for the consequences of those personal choices.

7:38 Nothing you do shall mean more to anyone more so than you.

7:39 No life is completely without faith.

7:40 No life is complete without faith.

7:41 Faith is complete; true faith is always complete.

7:42 Where life circumstance and tragedy shall happen, it is expected that a person with morality and of good character has a right to be angry and thus bitter towards society. Unforeseen death and brutality shall be mended partially by loss of spirit and care; it is to be expected; and for a short time accepted by others. "Why me?" To blame is warrant and blame towards others is expected, thou shall rely on faith to return to normal life, for life forever without normal behavior or routine is no positive life. Any life circumstance and tragedy should be overcome by you and the society in which you live, an ability to inspire a positive life. This positive life shall include you, your family and the society in which you live. When such tragedy happens to a person, others should encourage a common focal point to gain strong feelings toward themselves.

7:43 Life is a characteristic of physical events and activities with self-sustaining processes; those that do not have such functions, have to have acceptance of death, for death is also a part of faith.

7:44 Faith has absolutely no faults and faith is without impurities. People has faults and impurities.

7:45 Death without faith is final.

7:46 With faith, life is complete.

7:47 Have faith your life and life shall be with purpose and meaning.

END

7TH VERSE NOTES:

FAITH

8

8:1 Faith is having faith.

8:2 The higher being exists; a higher power exists.

8:3 Life is guided by the higher power, but standards of living is thine own responsibility.

8:4 No higher power will improve your furniture, running water, or bring you electricity. This power has been vested in you directly to achieve on your own. No prayer will bring you a brand new car or a visa to travel; it is your own labor and discipline to save your money to buy what you need.

8:5 Once you save the money, you shall pray for sound judgment and patience not to purchase the first car presented; seek the help of a professional.

8:6 You build your houses with cement which is very expensive; you shall not only build thou house with cement for in the western world, the land of milk and honey is blessed with riches and caring people known as Americans; they build their house of brick and wood. Some people in the western world build their entire house of wood and others brick.

8:7 The people often endure the harsh conditions of Mother Nature with 150 mile per hour winds and tropical rains, known as hurricanes and tornados; the ground can open and swallow you from earthquakes and the people continue to build with wood. Those houses built with wood, built by mothers and fathers who pass those same wooded houses for generations to their great, great grand-children, the same you can do.

8:8 Thou shall have a change of mind to know that prayer and worship gives strength; the strategy is accomplished with family, friends, professionals. Their house can also be built by the hammer and not just the masonry knife.

8:9 Thou shalt kneel on your knees and pray and once thou prayer is complete, thou shall go and do everything thou prayed for.

8:10 Prayer without work is just prayer; thinking that a prayer is heard without the work is just thinking.

8:11 Allow yourself to have an open mind to things you could never see with the human eye.

8:12 Believing in ghosts can say that there is proof of spiritual life, skeptics would argue they differ, but allow yourself to believe that a higher power is in all life forms, if you so choose.

8:13 You may have a gut feeling about something, or intuition which is to have a sixth sense, which can provide silent guidance.

8:14 Intuition can end distrust in someone, end a marriage, avoid a certain street, or steer you in any direction.

8:15 With no logical explanation, your intuition helps you make decisions, gives you confidence, and allows you to feel like you are making a good strong decision; this is based on a trusted power that is bigger than yourself; your intuition is something that you feel you never have to justify.

8:16 Strong belief can show you which way to go when the path is not clear.

8:17 If everything happens for a reason, then you must put forth the effort to ensure it happens for you.

8:18 Faith should bring out the best in you and help you bring out the best in others.

8:19 Faith, in some, takes a few days to obtain and others a lifetime.

8:20 Faith is wisdom, stability, focus, and peace.

END

8TH VERSE NOTES:

FAITH

ORIGINS

The Book of Raymond consists of 10 books:

1. Faith
2. Self (You)
3. Emotion
4. Professional
5. Relationship
6. Life/Death
7. Economic
8. People
9. Nature
10. Super Natural

While in Africa and South America, Dr. Raymond Youngblood, Jr. observed people's progression towards a better life. He simply noticed that no matter how much donor funding and no matter the non-profit programs, life was/is not getting better. As a matter fact, it was horrible in some places, downright horrible. How is this possible with so much donor funding pouring into these places? It's just not possible. But it's true! Why are people working so hard, yet nothing seems to get better in their life? They want improvements, but nobody seems to know what to do. The people don't know what to do and their governments don't know what to do. Diseases are running rampant, crime is rising and ending poverty seems hopeless. Somebody has to do something and something has to be done immediately. Where does a person need to start to fix things in an entire country?

Dr. Raymond Youngblood, Jr., a renowned international strategist, started to notice comprehension and comprehending weaknesses among certain groups of people. He is well known for his positive attitude towards life. Not that he was basing any of his findings of the issues described in psychological or medical listings, but something more within the culture; something that literally was making people content with the poverty; something that slowed their aggression towards improvement. This is not to deny mental health related issues, as it is blatantly visible among the population. Dr. Youngblood noticed that people copied every aspect of Western culture, but they often failed to grasp the root understanding of the societal working culture, language, development, and economics.

Other than fashion and entertainment, Dr. Youngblood observed that what was copied the most was worshiping.

People follow Western religious leaders and mimic the sense of style and services, but in a sense they never grasped the infrastructure of people and development. They lack applying what they learnt towards physical development.

The ten books were designed to complement Judaism, Islam, Christianity, Hinduism, Buddhism, Folk, Traditional and others forms of worship.

Dr. Youngblood started following and recording the people's love to worship and fellowship. One of the missing links to reducing poverty, ending killer diseases, and creating economic relief was prayer and praise. There is a problem and that is:

• Literacy (most of the people doing the praying can't even recognize their own name when they see it).

• Ignorance (most of the people believe that prayer and worship is all they need).

• Culture (built around primitive behavior and is not gender sensitive or modern).

• Economic (most of the people don't understand society and the relationship of economics to a society).

• Corruption (most people without a true understanding consciously/unconsciously support corruption).

- Human (most do not like their fellow citizens and are consistently jealous and evil acts against each other is often done).

Dr. Youngblood designed these books to truly be comprehended through traditional education, self-education and worship teachings. He believes that it is not possible to understand something fully without comprehending it fully. If instructions from religious leaders, government officials, and laws of the land, even with translation, are misunderstood, then it's not possible for the people to completely understand the tasks before them. It's not possible they can properly understand instructions. Often time problems rise and those same problems only escalate into more problems because the people are not developed or have too far to carry out a feeling or seek action on an act.

Dr. Youngblood would tell you he's not against uprising or war if the majority of citizens feel oppressed or enslaved or threatened with violence. He would tell the people there is a difference between majority of citizens being oppressed and a few angry citizens fighting for their own cause.

Dr. Youngblood, "Every cause doesn't deserve a fight, but ever fight deserves a cause, but a damn worthy cause."

It started with simple conversations with Dr. Youngblood's friends, and then with the instructions he gave his workers, his assisting government officials, and his attending various worship services. He observed that many people worship through the different formats of Churches, Temples, Mosques, Tents, Open Fields, etc. They would use the Bible, Karma, Quran, etc. and they use hymns, songs, scripture, quotes, etc. One fact became blatant; people still had no true concept of:

- Oneness, that togetherness is not within the people.

- Relinquishment, the people are not willing to try new and modern; they prefer to stick to the old ways, including the failures.

- Emotions, that there are different human emotions for various outcomes and situations.

- Mind and Spirit, the contextual meaning of faith as it applies to human development (prayer needs to be followed up with physical work).

- Economics, the transition of how the basic formalities of economics work in society (reaping what you sow).

- Expression of Feelings, the recognition and reaction to body language and facial expressions.

Believe it or not, these points are causing problems with cleanliness, negotiation of agreements, foreigners, following of governmental plans, corruption, onset and spread of disease, all of which is costing billions of dollars and thousands of lives. The people in poverty stricken countries are simply running their society on impassive behavior. The Pastors, Priests, Imams, Rabbis, etc. would provide great readings and instructions, but other than tithes, a true understanding of human concept is definitely missing.

Dr. Youngblood noticed the big separation in the religious messages from the actual content and teachings, (Bible, Quran, Karma, etc.) to the application to the people's daily life. He often attended the various worship centers and lives among the people in many different communities and villages. It seemed that the improvements only came through the worship centers and not directly to a person. As a worship service ended year after year, the society seems to have gotten worse. You can see false improvements when a skyscraper was erected, but ten years later that same building is dilapidated due to poor maintenance and planning. The more the money poured in, the worse the corruption and poverty.

After attending thousands of funerals, marriage vows, baptisms, and worship services he realized that many of the people attending, including the religious leaders, did not understand the basic language and meaning of situations they were teaching to their followers. They only knew customs and traditions, but it was never applied to societal improvements. For example, they would never fix the leak in the building; they just paint over it and later complain that water would drip on their heads. When the sun was out, they literally forgot the leak and praised how wonderful the paint made the building. This is a repetitive behavior over and over with everything in society. This happens with almost everything in society and almost everybody. If someone

attempted to fix the core problem, the community would chastise the person or become violent towards them. They continued to make the same mistakes to a new and old situation.

It is not possible that they can really understand what any religious message truly means when they do not know the meaning of fifty percent of the words they hear. When attending any worship service from any religious teaching, they never quite understand the utilization of adjectives, adverbs or past, present, or future tense. Dr. Youngblood thought that he would have to prove this to those helping these countries, but he soon realized that many of the people providing the help knew these things. They knew the people were not grasping the concepts, which is why poverty and disease still run rampant. Many of those claiming to help were only leaching, because to improve these societies would impact their budget of lavish spending and living. But, Youngblood feels differently. He believes that to improve the lesser society would greatly impact the stronger society. For example, if the U.S. got hands-on involved with physical, professional, and spiritual help to any Poor Nation, then the U.S. would gain more economically and spiritually than it could by just being a donor and depending on its large companies to reap financially. Yes, it's true that the taxes from these large U.S. companies greatly benefit the U.S., but the overall reward mostly benefits the companies, unless the companies became a part of the improvement. Not handouts! Improvements! If the companies partnered with the U.S. in these developments, the rewards economically would more than triple than what they currently profit. The reason being is that there is pressure on so many sellers and so many buyers; therefore,

you have the option to eliminate either market. This gives you all the power because no market exists unless you create it and those previous in the market will still be in need and in greater need. Is this possible just by improving someone's grammar or their understanding of present participle? There is a reason most successful companies hire the most successful professionals and students. The better you understand, the faster you can contribute, and contribute to the bottom line.

If the understanding of grammatical use is not understood by ninety percent of the population, it's impossible for improvements to happen or to take place.

Youngblood, "If you can't write, you can't read; if you can't read, you can't comprehend; if you can't comprehend, you can't communicate; if you can't communicate, you can't follow instructions; if you can't follow instructions, you can't improve and if you can't improve then…,"

This prompted Dr. Youngblood to write the ten books known as The Book Of Raymond.

NOT RELIGIOUSLY INTENDED

Though the ten books were never meant to be for worship, the teachings of the books are starting to go in that direction. The books, thought to be a canonical (sacred books) collection of texts and readings, the readers have expressed it to be a sacredness feeling toward the content. The Book Of Raymond includes different material divided with a combination of writings incorporating modernization, scientific study, physical action, human development, deeds, and faith with the principle of causality (cause and effect).

The Book Of Raymond is believed to be a new revelation with a scriptural style. It explains things so that people can apply content and phrases to their improvements. It is expanding among the international religious community and finding a major place within literature. It promotes good intentions, good deeds, and contributes to future happiness of people, while promoting and ending suffering from poverty, hatred, and ignorance.

Intended for Africa and South America, The Book of Raymond is undergoing a western transformation. All ten books are combined through a series. The books are divided into an Old Version and a New Version. When a book carries updates, additional material or deleted sections, it will carry the title New Version; therefore making the previous book the Old Version.

SAINT RAYMOND

Dr. Youngblood is the only international Black American Gold Miner on the planet It didn't seem likely that Dr. Youngblood could see himself as a Saint or definitely referred to as a Saint. A Saint, a person acknowledged as holy or virtuous and typically regarded as being in heaven after death, a Saint is one who has been recognized for having an exceptional degree of holiness. Dr. Youngblood would tell you that he's not dead and he's surely not holy enough to be a Saint. Even he admitted, he would feel offended when referred to as a Saint.

"I am a good human being, but not a Saint. I have had many physical fights; I have scarred the Earth; I have seen people die before my eyes and I know where they are still dying; I know of many wrong doings by 'good' people; therefore, I am not a Saint. Still people from all walks of life: Christians, Islamic, Hindu, Buddhist, Judaism, Juju, etc., like and love this me and what I can do for people."

What do these millions of people see in Dr. Youngblood? What has he done that they pray for him to be their leader; that they beg him to lead their leaders; without his knowledge, file for him to be a citizen of their country, hoping he would be their President?

"...he changed our life...,"

"...he saved us...,"

"...we were all going to die in this place...until he came...,"

"...he literally is changing this entire country, this is what makes him so great, he don't even know it."

MAKING CONNECTION

To not have an understanding of emotions and relationship between words, meaning and phrases, is frightening. Most Africans had not ever had an education about the different types of human emotions. This may be related to the barrier of the more than two thousands languages. The separation and differences between the meaning and uses of hate, evil, envy, and wicked are not applied.

The word "waste" is used for pour, squeeze, dash, etc. If I want water poured from the pan to the bucket, I can't say pour. I have to say waste the water from the pan to the bucket. This is a daily activity for most people in Africa. So imagine the context used for worship or even the laws. To use the word MIGHT or MAYBE in many African settings, might or maybe doesn't exist, it has no expression, and it has no meaning. You either can or cannot, you will or you will not, there is no in between. The word OF, though expressing the relationship between a part and a whole of something, in Africa the word "of" is not even properly understood and definitely not properly used and there are many others words and phrases that possess these same difficulties.

Then there are those elite people whom we regard as highly educated because they went to school in the U.S. or Europe. These same elite sometimes never grasp the concept either and they damn sure don't teach what they know to the people in their country.

How can so many people be living in such abject poverty?

But when it comes to praying, nobody, and I mean nobody, can pray better than these poor people. There is an old expression, "They can bring down the roof when they pray," but ask them to express the teaching and apply it to their standard of living, it becomes complex. They seem to only be able to repeat what they hear, but they don't understand and normally don't apply the message taught to improve their poverty level.

When Dr. Youngblood made the connection, he expressed that his mind started going in a thousand directions. He thought that his first improvement would be related to the disconnect between his workers and the instructions.

- To give instructions without the mistakes.

- Then explain to health practitioners the responsibilities of cleanliness and sanitation.

- Convincing citizens that their leaders need support without rebellion on every implementation of a plan.

- Create avenues for job development.

- Government officials to admit they don't know what to do to fix the country's problems, not get offended and then shut down emotionally.

After Dr. Youngblood spent significant time lecturing and researching with Christian, Muslim, and Hindu friends, the only solution they provided was to help the schools more. Dr. Youngblood expressed that trillions of dollars are pouring into African schools with the help of hundreds of Non-Profits/NGO's. That is not good enough. The everyday person is not going to school, because they spend their time hustling for food, medicine, and living space. There is something that everyone does no matter how poor or rich they are and that's go to worship and they go often. So, one of the best ways to reach people would be through the use of worship centers. Though these books started as an avenue to educate, Dr. Youngblood's workers and the people in the villages where he setup mining camps can now serve the masses. The first set of books was written more as talking points. Now they are more for the general public. He wrote the books to not matter if a person was a Buddhist, Christian, or Muslim, etc., because his miners represented all walks of life. Some of his workers were even reformed criminals being given a second or third chance by him. He would often say we must find a way to increase the intelligence of our people; they must become smarter if we are to grow this company and turn this village into a city. He believed that if the people were already learning from the multiple houses of worship, they must learn to progress. Prayer without effort is empty. They must learn simple human behavior, human develop-ment, and definitely human emotions. It is simple to understand how the people can understand that there is a difference in word usage and body language. They must learn that hate, bad, evil, jealousy, and wickedness have different meanings, as engineering is to architect.

It's all categorized the same and there is no one to tell them it's not the same and should be related to differently. This is not as simple as teaching basic phonics, language, and grammar. We are discussing change and change agents of culture.

Nevertheless, Dr. Youngblood just wanted to focus the books in a way that people understood and would apply to changing their mindset. Since many of them were already accustomed to the Bible, Quran, Karma, etc., he stayed with that type of structure: visual, word use and context. As you leaders teach from The Book Of Raymond, realize that it is meant to grow human beings, it is meant to help improve their living standards, and it is meant to better each other.

NAME: BOOK OF RAYMOND

The name, The Book Of Raymond, came from a set of 6 year old triplets living in a jungle mining camp. Dr. Youngblood started teaching village children how to play chess. He decided to work on adverbs, as adverbs are hard for Africans to understand. The first of the children he would meet every night were the triplets screaming and yelling, "Doctor, Doctor, we learn tonight!" "Of course," he said. He announced we would learn the working moves of the Rook and the defense of Pons. Sure enough when he said it, one of the triplets starting taunting, "Of course, Of Course, Of Course!" Later, one of the triplets asked, "Doctor, you going to teach us from the 'doctor's book." The way she said it made him laugh and he begin thinking that if he was going to write something, it had to be written in a way not to compete with the Bible, Quran, Karma, etc. It to be something that could help people understand with the basic essentials of life. Dr. Youngblood broke it down to cover basic human development.

1. FAITH
2. SELF(YOU)
3. EMOTION
4. PROFESSIONAL
5. RELATIONSHIP
6. LIFE/DEATH
7. ECONOMIC
8. PEOPLE
9. NATURE
10. SUPER NATURAL

He awoke from his sleep still laughing at the triplet referring to his teachings as 'Doctor's Book' but he converted it to The Book of Raymond.

ABOUT THE AUTHOR

Dr. Raymond Youngblood, Jr., Paramount Chief, Minerals Extractor (miner), Scientist, International Strategist, Author... He spends the majority of his time in Africa or South America.

"I noticed that the Africans and South Americans faith is strong and I wanted to help them with their understanding without being biased. One day I awoke with the ten books. What good will these things do for me if I cannot improve something or somebody? I want to use my skills as a miner, royalty as a Chief and experience as scientist to: Legalize Corruption in a way to move a country forward, Mine A Way Out Of Poverty with a country's using its existing minerals, Cut The Path To Development with the timber for building and manufacturing, Grow Out of Hunger with large scale agriculture from the reclamation of mining land, and stop diseases like Malaria, HIV/AIDS and Ebola by challenging cures to cultural adjustment. I spend a great deal of time in the Jungles and Deserts of Africa and South America...I know the jungle, I know the desert, and I know the Amazon and better yet, I know what it is capable of producing."

He's the only Black American Gold Miner on this planet and the only American holding the title of an African Paramount Chief with a Chieftaincy.

Dr. Youngblood currently lives between Africa, South America in the heart of the hot zones, and in the U.S. He is diverse in his relationship with international politicians, common citizens, elitists, and villagers. Credited for knowing more about Africans and South Americans than anyone other Westerner, his understanding of the African and South American environments and modern cultures goes deep into the cause of poverty, prolonging of diseases, and the relationship to corruption. He is a natural leader who is industry smart, with a keen reputation for being straight-forward. He is known as tenacious for having high standards, well connected, and a true team player. Dr. Youngblood is a Paramount Chief, an honor not customarily given to Americans, in the Republic of Liberia. He's an 'extreme micro' strategist who believes in getting it right the first time. Youngblood believes in being proactive and is a "cool head" in volatile situations. He spends a great deal of his time in villages and rural areas. He serves on the Board of Traditional Council of Chiefs & Elders. He remains at the top of his game both professionally and philanthropically in how he works in the rural areas. He knows every step a for-profit and non-profit should take to do business. He has worked with more than 5 million small and mid-scale gold and diamond miners. He is known in the Amazon and Jungles as the "Black Indiana Jones" and the "American Gold Miner." He is a well-seasoned business man and scientist with extreme hands-on experience in hostile and violent environments. He has strategic approaches to what he does. He was the original model and inspiration of today's Gold Mining Reality Shows. He is intelligent with his aggressive behavior and a natural strategic leader that is as brave as they come. Youngblood's entrepreneurial beginnings are rural develop-ment through mineral extractions. "His take the profits from the ground and build your way out of poverty approach is a key interest for African/South American leaders." He invented and was innovative with building mineral extraction machines and strategies. His uniquely aggressive business tactics and willingness to partner with like minds place him on the front lines with dedicated supporters. Other executives wanting to enter the lucrative and growing Africa/ South America markets can call on Youngblood for the approach. He's rugged, intelligent, and trustworthy, he live's there!

TRADITIONAL TITLES:
Paramount Chief Jallah Lone, Gbarpolu County, Republic of Liberia, Chieftaincy Region: Bopolu, Other Official Titles in Africa, India, South America

PROFESSION:
Mineral Extractor (Miner), International Business, Scientist, Inventor, Professor

RESIIDENTS:
United States, Liberia, Colombia

EXPERIENCE/ INVOLVEMENT:
22+ Years Africa & South America, Mining & Exploration, Value Added, Agriculture, Medical/Health, Timber, Goods & Services, Technology

FULLY ENGAGED:
Knowledge of Africa and South America Cultures, Amalgamation & Acquisitions, Negotiations, Extreme Hostile Work Environments, Operating in the Jungle, Desert & Amazon, Athletics, Land/ Business Development

EDUCATION:
Doctorate in International Business Administration, Master of Science in Management, Bachelor of Art in Psychology

PROFESSIONAL:
Six Sigma (G), Train the Trainer, Construction Management, Executive Training

KNOWN FOR:
"The Only Black American Gold Miner On The Planet," Working In Extreme Hostile Environments, Conflict Resolution, Ruggedly Tough, Straight-talker, Honesty

MINDSET:
Positive Thinker, High Standards, Aggressive, Strategic,

Creative, Natural Leader, Team
Orientated, No-nonsense

NATIONALITY:
American, United States

BIRTHPLACE:
Louisiana, United States

EXTENSIVE TRAVELS:
Africa, Asia, Central America,
Multiple Islands, North
America, South America

HOBBIES:
Creating/Inventing, Leadership
Development, Sports, Science
& Technology, Public
Speaking, Writing